THE
doughnut
COOKBOOK

DEVELOPED BY

WILLIAMS SONOMA

TEST KITCHEN

Photographs Eva Kolenko

weldon**owen**

Contents

coconut

strawberry

chocolate funfetti

vanilla funfetti

apple fritter

s'mores

lemon pistachio

vanilla
old-fashioned

maple-bacon

peppermint bark

cinnamon twist

All About Doughnuts

Whether glazed, sprinkled, jelly-filled, or dusted with sugar, doughnuts are a classic comfort food. Paired perfectly with a cup of steaming hot coffee or a glass of cold milk, these delectable sweets are fit for breakfast, dessert, or a special any-time treat. And they're easier to make than you might think. This comprehensive manual shows you how to prepare three basic varieties of doughnuts: yeasted, cake, and baked. With helpful tips and step-by-step photography outlining how to cut and fry, you'll be on your way to making bakery-quality doughnuts in the comfort of your home.

More than twenty recipes are included, featuring old-time favorites like crinkly-and-glazed Vanilla and Chocolate Old-Fashioned Doughnuts (pages 46 and 48), homey Apple Cider Doughnuts (page 42), confectioners' sugar–coated Beignets (page 36), and chocolate cream–filled Long John Doughnuts (page 30). If you crave filled doughnuts, you'll find plenty of great ideas for using chocolate-hazelnut spread, lemon curd, strawberry jelly, and blackberry-lemon jam as fillings. Discover exciting combinations like S'mores Doughnuts (page 34), Funfetti Doughnuts (page 45), Maple-Bacon Doughnuts (page 33), and more. With all of the baked doughnut recipes easily made gluten-free by substituting the same amount of gluten-free all-purpose flour, there really is something for everyone. You'll find all of these creative treats, as well as the classics you know and love, inside this inspiring volume.

The Three Types of Doughnuts

This book divides doughnuts into three different types: yeasted, cake, and baked. Each type of dough, whether fried or baked, produces doughnuts with a different texture and density.

Yeasted Doughnuts

Using yeast as a leavener results in light, fluffy, and chewy doughnuts from multiple rises. It's important to plan for extra time for these steps; skimping on the rising time will make the doughnut too airy. Yeasted dough can be refrigerated overnight for the first or second rise. Bring it to room temperature before rolling and frying.

Cake Doughnuts

Leavened by baking powder and baking soda, cake doughnuts are denser than yeasted ones and often have a crusty exterior. The preparation time is much shorter than for yeasted doughnuts. Keep in mind that the dough can be very sticky, so knead it on a well-floured surface but just until combined—do not overknead. It's important to roll out the dough just to the specified thickness in the recipe. Otherwise the doughnuts will be dense and tough. The sticky dough creates the perfect doughnut crumb.

Baked Doughnuts

These are made with a liquidy batter that is poured into a molded doughnut pan and then baked. The doughnuts are lighter, fluffier, and healthier than their fried counterparts. Baked doughnuts can be flavored with a variety of spices and toppings, such as cinnamon-sugar, glazes, and chopped nuts.

TOPPINGS GALORE

Sweet or savory, crunchy or chewy, there are endless treats that can be used to top doughnuts. Crush larger ingredients and use miniature versions of toppings when available. These ideas will get you started. Use any flavor glaze to help the toppings adhere.

- potato chips
- cereal
- popcorn
- cookies
- pretzels
- toffee
- coconut flakes
- toasted nuts
- crystallized ginger
- shaved chocolate
- mini candies
- edible rose petals
- dried fruit
- multicolor sprinkles
- miniature marshmallows

Tips & Tricks for Cutting Doughnuts

Doughnuts can be cut into all sorts of shapes and sizes, from traditional rings to "holes," fritters, long johns, and more. Remember that increasing or decreasing the size of your doughnuts will affect the cooking time.

For yeasted doughnuts, use a 3½-inch round cutter (pastry ring) plus a 1-inch pastry ring to cut the holes in the center or a doughnut cutter. Roll out the dough to ½-inch thickness.

For cake doughnuts, use a 3-inch round cutter plus a 1-inch pastry ring for the holes or a doughnut cutter. Roll out the dough to ½-inch thickness.

For baked doughnuts, use a doughnut pan. (You can find these at Williams Sonoma, both in the stores and online.) Be sure to coat the wells of the pan with nonstick cooking spray before filling them with batter.

To create the iconic tapered edges that are the hallmark of old-fashioned doughnuts, cut three slits on top of the uncooked doughnut dough, which should create a triangle shape on top of the doughnut after frying.

After cutting out yeasted and cake doughnuts, reroll the leftover dough only once. Otherwise, you'll end up with tough doughnuts.

The image above shows what an old fashioned doughnut looks like before frying (see instructions at left).

How to Fry Doughnuts

Frying doughnuts is a cinch when you follow these guidelines.

Successful Frying
Set a cooling rack or a baking sheet lined with paper towels nearby.
Fill a large, deep pot halfway with oil. Heat over medium-high until it
registers the recipe's frying temperature on a deep-frying thermometer
(for yeasted doughnuts, 310–325°F; for cake doughnuts, 360°F). Adjust
the heat to maintain the temperature. Working in small batches, carefully
place the doughnuts and holes in the oil. Fry, turning once, until lightly
golden brown and cooked through (cut one open to test; see recipes
for frying times).

1. Opt for a Large Pot
Always fry in a large, deep pot, like a 5-quart Dutch oven, filled no more
than half full to decrease the chance of oil spilling or bubbling over.

2. Use Neutral-Flavored Oil and Reuse When You Can
Always use oil with a high smoke point or a neutral-flavored oil that can
be heated smoke-free for a long time. In the Williams Sonoma Test
Kitchen, our first choice is canola oil, but vegetable, corn, peanut, and
sunflower oils work well, too. Most oil can be used at least twice for
frying. If the oil is murky, discard it in a container; if it is clear, reuse it
until murky. When you are done frying the doughnuts, let the oil come
to room temperature. Strain it back into its original container using
a sieve set over a funnel.

3. Stabilize the Temperature
Maintaining the correct temperature is crucial to frying doughnuts.
To make that easy, invest in a deep-frying thermometer that clips to
the side of the pot.

Classic Glazes

Here is a trio of easy-to-make glazes for dressing up your doughnuts. Once the glaze is applied, be sure to gild with any garnishes—sprinkles, toasted nuts, shredded coconut, chocolate chips—before it sets.

VANILLA GLAZE

2 cups confectioners' sugar

½ teaspoon salt

½ cup whole milk

2 teaspoons vanilla extract

CHOCOLATE GLAZE

¼ cup hot water

¼ lb semisweet chocolate

1½ teaspoons vanilla extract

2 cups confectioners' sugar

5 tablespoons unsalted butter

¼ teaspoon salt

STRAWBERRY GLAZE

½ cup strawberry syrup (see page 51)

2 cups confectioners' sugar

Pinch of salt

Vanilla Glaze

In a bowl, stir together the confectioners' sugar, salt, milk, and vanilla until smooth and well blended. (Reduce the amount of milk for a thicker glaze.) Stir gently before glazing the doughnuts. Use the glaze within an hour or cover and refrigerate for up to 3 days.

Chocolate Glaze

Fill a small saucepan with 2 inches of water and bring to a gentle simmer over low heat. Place a medium bowl over but not touching the water. In the bowl, combine the hot water, chocolate, vanilla, confectioners' sugar, butter, and salt. (Reduce the amount of water for a thicker glaze.) Cook, stirring occasionally, until the chocolate and butter are melted, 2–3 minutes. Remove from the heat and stir until smooth and well blended. Cover the bowl with plastic wrap to keep warm until the doughnuts are ready to glaze, or cover and refrigerate for up to 3 days. Gently reheat in the bowl over the saucepan or in a microwave-safe bowl in the microwave for 20–30 seconds before using.

Strawberry Glaze

Make the strawberry syrup as directed on page 51, reserving ½ cup of the syrup for the glaze. In a bowl, stir together the confectioners' sugar, strawberry syrup, and salt until smooth and well blended. Stir gently before glazing the doughnuts. Use the glaze within an hour or cover and refrigerate for up to 3 days.

Basic Yeast Doughnuts

These airy, fluffy, slightly—and pleasantly—"stretchy" doughnuts are a mainstay of the American doughnut shop. Also known as raised doughnuts, they turn up in a variety of shapes: rings, disks, twists, and logs.

1 cup warm whole milk (110–120°F)

2¼ teaspoons instant yeast

3 tablespoons vegetable shortening, melted and cooled slightly

1 large egg

¼ cup sugar

2 teaspoons salt

3 cups all-purpose flour, plus more for dusting

Canola oil, for greasing and frying

Glaze, as desired

Pour the warm milk into a small bowl, sprinkle the yeast on top, and stir gently. Let stand in a warm spot until foamy, 5–10 minutes.

Transfer the yeast mixture to the bowl of a stand mixer fitted with the paddle attachment. Add the shortening, egg, sugar, salt, and 1½ cups of the flour and beat on low speed until combined, about 2 minutes. Add the remaining 1½ cups flour, raise the speed to medium, and beat until incorporated, about 30 seconds. Switch to the dough hook and beat on medium speed until the dough is smooth and pulls away from the bowl, 3-4 minutes. Transfer to a well-oiled bowl, cover with plastic wrap or a kitchen towel, and let the dough rise in a warm spot until doubled in size, about 1 hour.

Punch down the dough, turn it out onto a well-floured work surface, and roll out ½ inch thick. Using a doughnut cutter or 2 different-sized round cutters (3½ inch and 1 inch), cut out doughnuts and holes. Transfer to a well-floured baking sheet, cover lightly with plastic wrap or a kitchen towel, and let rise in a warm spot until doubled in size, about 1 hour.

To fry the doughnuts, see Successful Frying (page 14). Heat the oil over medium-high until it registers 325°F on a deep-frying thermometer. When the doughnuts are cooked through (cut one open to test), 1–2 minutes per side (holes take less time), use a slotted spoon to transfer to a cooling rack or prepared baking sheet. Let cool for 10 minutes before glazing.

AFTER THE FIRST rise, the punched-down dough can be stored overnight in the refrigerator. Let stand at room temperature for 20 minutes before rolling and cutting the doughnuts.

Salted Caramel Doughnuts

What started as salted caramel candies in Brittany has blossomed into a mini industry of salted caramel–flavored ice cream, sauce, cakes, and now doughnuts. *Fleur de sel* or Maldon sea salt is a good choice here.

1 recipe Vanilla Old-Fashioned Doughnuts (page 46)

1½ cups sugar

1 teaspoon fresh lemon juice

1½ cups heavy cream

1½ teaspoons flaky sea salt, plus more for garnish

Canola oil, for frying

Make the vanilla doughnut dough and knead. Roll it out to ½-inch thickness, cut out doughnuts and holes, and refrigerate.

Meanwhile, in a saucepan, stir together the sugar, lemon juice, and ¼ cup water. Place over medium heat and cook, stirring continuously, until the mixture bubbles vigorously and turns a golden amber color, 7–9 minutes. Remove from the heat and immediately and very carefully add the cream; the mixture will bubble and splatter. Stir until the sauce is smooth, then stir in the sea salt. Let cool until warm.

To fry the doughnuts, see Successful Frying (page 14). Heat the oil over medium-high until it registers 360°F on a deep-frying thermometer. When the doughnuts are cooked through (cut one open to test), 1–2 minutes per side (holes take less time), use a slotted spoon to transfer to a cooling rack or prepared baking sheet. Let cool for 5 minutes. Dip the doughnuts, top side down, into the caramel sauce. Garnish with sea salt and serve.

THE CINNAMON TWISTS will untwist once while frying, so overlapping the strips of dough three times will ensure a classic twist.

Cinnamon Twists

Make a batch of these popular cinnamon-and-sugar-coated twists for a leisurely Sunday morning breakfast with friends or neighbors. Serve them warm, accompanied by fresh fruit, yogurt, and a choice of coffee or tea.

1 recipe Basic Yeast Doughnuts (page 18)

⅔ cup sugar

2 teaspoons ground cinnamon

Pinch of salt

All-purpose flour, for dusting

Canola oil, for frying

Make the yeast doughnut dough and let rise until doubled in size, about 1 hour. Meanwhile, in a small bowl, stir together the sugar, cinnamon, and salt. Spread the mixture out on a large plate or a baking sheet. Set aside.

Punch down the dough, turn it out onto a well-floured work surface, and roll out into a 12-by-8-inch rectangle about ½ inch thick. Cut the dough into 8-by-1½-inch rectangles, then cut each rectangle in half lengthwise, leaving ½ inch at the top connected. Fold the left strip over the top of the right, then overlap the strips 2 more times. Pinch the ends together to seal. Transfer to a well-floured baking sheet, cover lightly with plastic wrap or a kitchen towel, and let rise in a warm spot until doubled in size, about 1 hour.

To fry the twists, see Successful Frying (page 14). Heat the oil over medium-high heat until it registers 325°F on a deep-frying thermometer. When the twists are cooked through (cut one open to test), 3–4 minutes per side, use a slotted spoon to transfer to a cooling rack or prepared baking sheet. Let cool for 5 minutes. Toss the twists in the sugar-cinnamon mixture and serve warm.

Apple Fritters

If you cannot find Granny Smiths, choose another tart-sweet, firm apple, such as Pippin, Rome Beauty, or Jonagold for these fruity fritters. If pressed for time, skip the glaze and sprinkle with confectioners' sugar.

1 recipe Basic Yeast Doughnuts (page 18)

2 apples, preferably Granny Smith, peeled, cored, and cut into ¼-inch dice

1 teaspoon fresh lemon juice

1½ tablespoons unsalted butter

1 teaspoon ground cinnamon

2 pinches of salt

1 tablespoon cornstarch

3 cups confectioners' sugar

½ cup plus 1 tablespoon apple juice

All-purpose flour, for dusting

Canola oil, for frying

Make the yeast doughnut dough and let rise until doubled in size, about 1 hour. Meanwhile, in a saucepan, combine the apples, lemon juice, butter, cinnamon, and a pinch of salt over medium-high heat and cook, stirring occasionally, until the apples are tender, about 5 minutes. Remove from the heat and stir in the cornstarch. Refrigerate until cool.

In a bowl, whisk together the confectioners' sugar, apple juice, and a pinch of salt. Set the glaze aside.

Punch down the dough, turn it out onto a well-floured work surface, and roll out into a 14-by-10-inch rectangle about ½ inch thick. Scatter three-fourths of the apples over the dough and roll into a long log. Flatten the log slightly and scatter the remaining apples on top. Starting with a short side, roll up the log into a large ball. Using a rolling pin, roll out into a 7½ x 10-inch rectangle about ½ inch thick. If apple pieces fall out, place back in the dough when shaping the fritters. Cut the dough into twelve 2½-inch squares. Pull the corners of each square toward the center. Place on a parchment-lined baking sheet. Let rise in a warm spot, covered, until almost doubled in size, about 30 minutes.

To fry the fritters, see Successful Frying (page 14). Heat the oil over medium-high until it registers 325°F on a deep-frying thermometer. When the fritters are cooked through (cut one open to test), 7–9 minutes per side, use a slotted spoon to transfer to a cooling rack or prepared baking sheet. Let cool for 5 minutes. Toss the fritters in the glaze and serve warm.

DON'T WORRY ABOUT making each apple fritter uniform in shape. Once fried, the dough takes on a craggy form, with lots of cracks for holding extra glaze.

Chocolate Hazelnut–Filled Doughnuts

The classic creamy mix of cocoa, milk, sugar, and hazelnuts is hard to resist after your first bite of these cinnamon sugar–dusted gems. Squeeze the pastry bag gently so the filling evenly floods the doughnut's heart.

1 recipe Basic Yeast Doughnuts (page 18)

3 tablespoons heavy cream

1½ cups chocolate hazelnut spread

½ cup sugar

½ teaspoon ground cinnamon

All-purpose flour, for dusting

Canola oil, for frying

Make the yeast doughnut dough and let rise until doubled in size, about 1 hour. Meanwhile, in a bowl, whisk the cream until soft peaks form. Gently stir in the chocolate hazelnut spread until combined. Cover and refrigerate the filling until ready to use.

In a bowl, stir together the sugar and cinnamon. Set aside.

Punch down the dough, turn it out onto a well-floured work surface, and roll out ½ inch thick. Using a 2½-inch round cutter, cut out doughnuts. Transfer to a well-floured baking sheet, cover lightly with plastic wrap or a kitchen towel, and let rise in a warm spot until doubled in size, about 1 hour.

To fry the doughnuts, see Successful Frying (page 14). Heat the oil over medium-high heat until it registers 310-320°F on a deep-frying thermometer. When the doughnuts are cooked through (cut one open to test), 3-4 minutes per side, use a slotted spoon to transfer to a cooling rack or prepared baking sheet. Let cool for 15 minutes.

Transfer the filling to a pastry bag and cut a ¼-inch opening. Using a small, sharp knife, cut a slit into the side and extending into the center of each doughnut. Insert the cut tip into the slit to the center and pipe in a generous 1 tablespoon filling. Gently toss the doughnuts in the sugar-cinnamon mixture and serve.

Lemon Curd–Filled Doughnuts

Any of your favorite citrus curds—grapefruit, orange, tangerine, lime—can replace the lemon curd used here. To heighten the lemon flavor, stir in 1 teaspoon finely grated zest after passing the curd through a sieve.

1 recipe Basic Yeast
Doughnuts (page 18)

4 large egg yolks

¼ cup granulated sugar

¼ cup fresh lemon juice

4 tablespoons
unsalted butter

Pinch of salt

All-purpose flour,
for dusting

Canola oil, for frying

½ cup confectioners' sugar

Make the yeast doughnut dough and let rise until doubled in size, about 1 hour. Meanwhile, in a small saucepan, combine the egg yolks, granulated sugar, lemon juice, butter, and salt. Cook over low heat, whisking frequently, until the mixture thickens, 10–15 minutes. Pour the lemon curd through a fine-mesh sieve into a bowl. Let cool to room temperature, then cover and refrigerate.

Punch down the dough, turn it out onto a well-floured work surface, and roll out ½ inch thick. Using a 2½-inch round cutter, cut out doughnuts. Transfer to a well-floured baking sheet, cover lightly with plastic wrap or a kitchen towel, and let rise in a warm spot until doubled in size, about 1 hour.

To fry the doughnuts, see Successful Frying (page 14). Heat the oil over medium-high until it registers 310–320°F on a deep-frying thermometer. When the doughnuts are cooked through (cut one open to test), 3–4 minutes per side, use a slotted spoon to transfer to a cooling rack or prepared baking sheet. Let cool for 15 minutes.

Transfer the curd to a pastry bag and cut a ¼-inch opening. Using a small, sharp knife, cut a slit into the side and extending into the center of each doughnut. Insert the cut tip into the slit to the center and pipe in a generous 1 tablespoon curd. Lightly dust the doughnuts with confectioners' sugar and serve.

Chocolate Long John Doughnuts

These bar-shaped doughnuts boast a double treat: a chocolate cream filling and a chocolate glaze. East Coast aficionados switch it up, opting for a custard or cream filling, a maple glaze (page 33), and a new name: maple bars.

1 recipe Basic Yeast
Doughnuts (page 18)

½ lb bittersweet chocolate,
roughly chopped

1¾ cups heavy cream

Pinch of salt

All-purpose flour,
for dusting

Canola oil, for frying

1 recipe Chocolate
Glaze (page 17)

Flaky sea salt

Make the yeast doughnut dough and let rise until doubled in size, about 1 hour. Meanwhile, place the chocolate in the bowl of a stand mixer fitted with the whisk attachment. In a small saucepan over medium-high heat, warm the cream until barely simmering. Pour over the chocolate and let stand until melted, 5–7 minutes. Sprinkle with salt and whisk until the chocolate is melted. Refrigerate until cool.

Punch down the dough, turn it out onto a well-floured work surface, and roll out into a 14-by-12-inch rectangle about ½ inch thick. Cut into 12 rectangles, each 6 inches long. Transfer to a well-floured baking sheet, cover lightly with plastic wrap or a kitchen towel, and let rise in a warm spot until doubled in size, about 1 hour.

To fry the doughnuts, see Successful Frying (page 14). Heat the oil over medium-high until it registers 325°F on a deep-frying thermometer. When the doughnuts are cooked through (cut one open to test), 4–6 minutes per side, use a slotted spoon to transfer to the cooling rack or prepared baking sheet. Let cool for 15 minutes.

Return the chocolate cream to the mixer fitted with the whisk attachment. Beat on medium speed until beginning to thicken, 20–30 seconds. Let stand for 5 minutes. Transfer to a pastry bag and cut a ¼-inch opening. Pipe 2–3 tablespoons chocolate cream into each doughnut. Dip the doughnuts, top side down, into the glaze. Sprinkle with sea salt and serve.

FOR PEANUT BUTTER cup flavors, sprinkle toasted and finely chopped peanuts over the chocolate glaze.

MAPLE EXTRACT
can be found in the
baking aisle of most
grocery stores. You can
try substituting rum
extract for the maple.

Maple-Bacon Doughnuts

Choose a high-quality bacon, like applewood or hickory-smoked, for this recipe that pairs two familiar morning flavors: crisply cooked bacon and sweet maple syrup.

1 recipe Basic Yeast
Doughnuts (page 18)

¼ lb bacon, diced

1½ cups confectioners'
sugar

3 tablespoons whole milk

2 teaspoons maple extract

All-purpose flour,
for dusting

Canola oil, for frying

Make the yeast doughnut dough and let rise until doubled in size, about 1 hour. Meanwhile, in a small frying pan over medium heat, cook the bacon until crispy, 4–6 minutes. Transfer to a paper towel–lined plate. Let cool, then roughly chop.

In a bowl, whisk together the confectioners' sugar, milk, and maple extract until smooth and well blended. Set aside.

Punch down the dough, turn it out onto a well-floured work surface, and roll out ½ inch thick. Using a doughnut cutter or 2 different-sized round cutters (3½ inch and 1 inch), cut out doughnuts and holes. Transfer to a well-floured baking sheet, cover lightly with plastic wrap or a kitchen towel, and let rise in a warm spot until doubled in size, about 1 hour.

To fry the doughnuts, see Successful Frying (page 14). Heat the oil over medium-high heat until it registers 325°F on a deep-frying thermometer. When the doughnuts are cooked through (cut one open to test), 1–2 minutes per side (the holes take less time), use a slotted spoon to transfer to a cooling rack or prepared baking sheet. Let cool for 5 minutes.

Dip the doughnuts, top side down, into the glaze. Sprinkle each with about 1 tablespoon bacon and serve.

S'mores Doughnuts

Here, the campfire classic is deconstructed with delicious results: a split doughnut sandwiches toasted marshmallows and is topped with chocolate glaze and graham cracker crumbs. For an Italian touch, substitute biscotti or amaretti crumbs.

1 recipe Vanilla Old-Fashioned Doughnuts (page 46)

1 recipe Chocolate Glaze (page 17)

½ cup confectioners' sugar

Canola oil, for frying

20–24 marshmallows

1 cup crushed graham crackers

Flaky sea salt (optional)

Make the vanilla doughnut dough and knead. Roll it out, cut out doughnuts and holes, and refrigerate.

Meanwhile, make the chocolate glaze and then stir in an additional ½ cup confectioners' sugar. Keep warm until ready to glaze the doughnuts.

To fry the doughnuts, see Successful Frying (page 14). Heat the oil over medium-high until it registers 360°F on a deep-frying thermometer. When the doughnuts are cooked through (cut one open to test), 1–2 minutes per side (holes will take less time), use a slotted spoon to transfer to a cooling rack or prepared baking sheet. Let cool for 5 minutes. Cut the doughnuts in half horizontally.

To assemble each doughnut, toast 2 marshmallows over an open flame until golden brown, 1–2 minutes. Place on the cut side of a doughnut half. Dip the uncut side of the other doughnut half into the glaze, then place, cut side down, on top of the marshmallows to form a sandwich. Sprinkle crushed graham crackers over the chocolate, garnish with sea salt, if using, and serve.

A KITCHEN TORCH or a gas burner is a great way to toast the marshmallows if you don't have a campfire handy.

Beignets

Dusted lavishly with confectioners' sugar and served piping hot, these light, puffy golden squares are perfect paired with a morning café au lait or with a late-night hot chocolate.

1 cup warm water
(110–120°F)

2¼ teaspoons
instant yeast

3 tablespoons vegetable
shortening, melted
and cooled slightly

1 large egg

¼ cup granulated sugar

2 teaspoons salt

3 cups all-purpose flour,
plus more for dusting

Canola oil, for
greasing and frying

2 cups confectioners'
sugar

Pour the warm water into a small bowl, sprinkle the yeast on top, and stir gently. Let stand in a warm spot until foamy, 5–10 minutes.

Transfer the yeast mixture to the bowl of a stand mixer fitted with the paddle attachment. Add the shortening, egg, granulated sugar, salt, and 1½ cups of the flour and beat on low speed until combined, about 2 minutes. Add the remaining 1½ cups flour, raise the speed to medium, and beat until incorporated, about 30 seconds. Switch to the dough hook and beat on medium speed until the dough is smooth and pulls away from the bowl, 3–4 minutes. Transfer to a well-oiled bowl, cover with plastic wrap or a kitchen towel, and let the dough rise in a warm spot until doubled in size, about 1 hour.

Punch down the dough, turn it out onto a well-floured work surface, and roll out ¼ inch thick. Cut into 2-inch squares. Transfer to a well-floured baking sheet, cover lightly with plastic wrap or a kitchen towel, and let rise in a warm spot until doubled in size, about 1 hour.

To fry the doughnuts, see Successful Frying (page 14). Heat the oil over medium-high until it registers 325°F on a deep-frying thermometer. When the beignets are cooked through (cut one open to test), 1–2 minutes per side, use a slotted spoon to transfer to a cooling rack or prepared baking sheet. When cool enough to handle, dust with confectioners' sugar and serve.

Blackberry-Lemon Jam–Filled Doughnuts

Jam– and jelly–filled doughnuts are typically treated to a dusting of confectioners' sugar. But you can instead use superfine sugar or vanilla sugar (to make, bury 1 or 2 vanilla beans in 2 cups of sugar for 2 weeks).

1 recipe Basic Yeast Doughnuts (page 18)

½ lb fresh or frozen blackberries, thawed if frozen

1 cup granulated sugar

Zest and juice of 1 lemon

¼ teaspoon salt

All-purpose flour, for dusting

Canola oil, for frying

½ cup confectioners' sugar

Make the yeast doughnut dough and let rise until doubled in size, about 1 hour. Meanwhile, in a bowl, toss together the blackberries and granulated sugar; let stand for 20 minutes. Transfer to a small saucepan, add the lemon zest and juice and salt, and cook over low heat, stirring frequently, until thickened, 20-25 minutes. Transfer to a bowl, let cool to room temperature, cover, and refrigerate until ready to use. For a smoother consistency, strain the jam through a fine-mesh sieve.

Punch down the dough, turn it out onto a well-floured work surface, and roll out ½ inch thick. Using a 2½-inch round cutter, cut out doughnuts. Transfer to a well-floured baking sheet, cover lightly with plastic wrap or a kitchen towel, and let rise in a warm spot until doubled in size, about 1 hour.

To fry the doughnuts, see Successful Frying (page 14). Heat the oil over medium-high until it registers 310-320°F on a deep-frying thermometer. When the doughnuts are cooked through (cut one open to test), 3-4 minutes per side, use a slotted spoon to transfer to a cooling rack or prepared baking sheet. Let cool for 15 minutes.

Transfer the jam to a pastry bag and cut a ¼-inch opening. Using a small, sharp knife, cut a slit into the side and extending into the center of each doughnut. Insert the cut tip into the slit to the center and pipe in a generous 1 tablespoon jam. Dust with confectioners' sugar and serve.

Peanut Butter and Jelly Doughnuts

MAKES ABOUT 10–12 3" DOUGHNUTS

Both grown-ups and kids are guaranteed to like this imaginative twist on America's iconic lunch box sandwich. To increase the nut flavor, sprinkle the freshly glazed doughnuts with double the chopped salted peanuts.

1 recipe Basic Yeast
Doughnuts (page 18)

1½ cups confectioners'
sugar

6 tablespoons whole milk

¼ cup smooth
peanut butter

Pinch of salt

All-purpose flour,
for dusting

Canola oil, for frying

¾ cup strawberry jelly

¼ cup salted peanuts,
toasted and finely chopped

Flaky sea salt

Make the yeast doughnut dough and let rise until doubled in size, about 1 hour. Meanwhile, in a bowl, whisk together the confectioners' sugar, milk, peanut butter, and salt until smooth and well blended. Set the glaze aside.

Punch down the dough, turn it out onto a well-floured work surface, and roll out ½ inch thick. Using a 2½-inch round cutter, cut out doughnuts. Transfer to a well-floured baking sheet, cover lightly with plastic wrap or a kitchen towel, and let rise in a warm spot until doubled in size, about 1 hour.

To fry the doughnuts, see Successful Frying (page 14). Heat the oil over medium-high until it registers 325°F on a deep-frying thermometer. When the doughnuts are cooked through (cut one open to test), 1–2 minutes per side, use a slotted spoon to transfer to a cooling rack or prepared baking sheet. Let cool for 15 minutes.

Transfer the jelly to a pastry bag and cut a ¼-inch opening. Using a small, sharp knife, cut a slit into the side and extending into the center of each doughnut. Insert the cut tip into the slit to the center and pipe in 1–2 tablespoons jelly into each doughnut. Dip, top side down, into the glaze. Sprinkle with peanuts and a pinch of sea salt and serve.

Coconut Doughnuts

To deepen the coconut flavor, substitute 1½ teaspoons coconut extract for 1½ teaspoons of the vanilla extract in the doughnut dough. For a shaggier finish, use shredded dried coconut in place of the coconut flakes.

---

1 recipe Vanilla Old-Fashioned Doughnuts (page 46)

⅔ cup coconut flakes

1 cup coconut milk

3 cups confectioners' sugar

2 teaspoons light corn syrup (optional)

½ teaspoon coconut extract (optional)

Canola oil, for frying

Make the vanilla doughnut dough and knead. Roll it out to ½-inch thickness, cut out doughnuts and holes, and refrigerate.

Meanwhile, preheat the oven to 350°F. Spread the coconut flakes in an even layer on a baking sheet. Bake until the edges are golden brown and toasted, 6–8 minutes. Let cool.

In a bowl, stir together the coconut milk and confectioners' sugar until smooth and well blended. For a shinier glaze, stir in the corn syrup. For extra coconut flavor, stir in the coconut extract. Set aside.

To fry the doughnuts, see Successful Frying (page 14). Heat the oil over medium-high until it registers 360°F on a deep-frying thermometer. When the doughnuts are cooked through (cut one open to test), 1–2 minutes per side (holes take less time), use a slotted spoon to transfer to a cooling rack or prepared baking sheet. Let cool for 5 minutes. Dip the doughnuts, top side down, into the glaze. Sprinkle with the coconut flakes and serve.

IF COCONUT MILK is not readily available for the glaze, substitute with the vanilla glaze recipe (page 17) and add a couple drops of coconut extract.

Apple Cider Doughnuts

MAKES ABOUT 14–16 3" DOUGHNUTS

Crusty on the outside and moist on the inside, these traditional sweet-spicy cake doughnuts are popular in Northeast apple country. Be sure to use robust, earthy-flavored unfiltered and unsweetened apple cider.

1 cup unfiltered
apple cider

1 cinnamon stick

3½ cups all-purpose flour,
plus more for dusting

1 tablespoon
baking powder

1¼ teaspoons baking soda

1 teaspoon salt

2 teaspoons ground
cinnamon

½ cup buttermilk

6 tablespoons unsalted
butter, melted and cooled

2 large eggs

1½ cups granulated sugar

½ cup firmly packed
light brown sugar

Canola oil, for frying

In a small saucepan, combine the apple cider and cinnamon stick over high heat and boil until reduced to about ⅓ cup, 12–15 minutes. Let cool. Discard the cinnamon stick.

In a bowl, whisk together the flour, baking powder, baking soda, salt, and 1 teaspoon of the ground cinnamon. Set aside.

In the bowl of a stand mixer fitted with the paddle attachment, beat together the cider, buttermilk, butter, eggs, ½ cup of the granulated sugar, and the brown sugar on medium speed until well combined. Add the flour mixture and beat until a dough forms.

Turn the dough out onto a well-floured surface and roll out ½ inch thick. Using a doughnut cutter or 2 different-sized round cutters (3 inch and 1 inch), cut out doughnuts and holes. Transfer to a well-floured baking sheet. Repeat with the scraps. Reroll only once; otherwise, the doughnuts will be tough. Refrigerate for 30 minutes before frying or up to 2 hours.

To fry the doughnuts, see Successful Frying (page 14). Heat the oil over medium-high until it registers 360°F on a deep-frying thermometer. When the doughnuts are cooked through (cut one open to test), 1–2 minutes per side (holes take less time), use a slotted spoon to transfer to a cooling rack or prepared baking sheet. Let cool for 5 minutes.

In a shallow bowl, stir together the remaining 1 cup granulated sugar and 1 teaspoon ground cinnamon. Toss the doughnuts in the mixture and serve.

Carrot Cake Doughnuts

These carrot cake–inspired doughnuts are irresistible. To continue the carrot cake theme, top the glaze with a scattering of chopped pecans. Shred the carrots with a food processor or on the fine holes of a box grater.

FOR THE DOUGHNUTS

3 cups all-purpose flour, plus more for dusting

1 teaspoon *each* salt and baking powder

½ teaspoon *each* baking soda, ground allspice, and ground cinnamon

2 tablespoons unsalted butter, melted and cooled

3 teaspoons vanilla extract

2 large eggs

½ cup buttermilk

½ cup *each* granulated sugar and firmly packed light brown sugar

1 cup finely shredded carrots

FOR THE GLAZE

1⅓ cups confectioners' sugar

4 oz cream cheese, at room temperature

¼ teaspoon *each* vanilla extract and salt

2 tablespoons whole milk

Canola oil, for frying

To make the doughnuts, in a bowl, whisk together the flour, salt, baking powder, baking soda, allspice, and cinnamon. In a measuring cup, stir together the butter and vanilla. Set aside.

In the bowl of a stand mixer fitted with the paddle attachment, beat together the eggs, buttermilk, and sugars on medium until well combined. Using a paper towel, squeeze any moisture from the carrots, then add to the egg mixture and beat on medium speed until combined, about 1 minute. Add the flour mixture and beat until just combined, then beat in the butter mixture until just combined.

Turn the dough out onto a well-floured surface and knead until the dough comes together. Roll out ½ inch thick. Using a doughnut cutter or 2 different-sized round cutters (3 inch and 1 inch), cut out doughnuts and holes. Transfer to a well-floured baking sheet and refrigerate for at least 30 minutes or up to 2 hours.

Meanwhile, make the glaze: In a bowl, whisk together the confectioners' sugar, cream cheese, vanilla, and salt. Add the milk and stir until smooth.

To fry the doughnuts, see Successful Frying (page 14). Heat the oil over medium-high until it registers 360°F on a deep-frying thermometer. When the doughnuts are cooked through (cut one open to test), 1–2 minutes per side (holes take less time), use a slotted spoon to transfer to a cooling rack or prepared baking sheet. Let cool for 5 minutes. Dip the doughnuts, top side down, into the glaze and serve.

Funfetti Doughnuts

These festive vanilla doughnuts call for sprinkles both in the batter and as a garnish. Also known as nonpareils and jimmies, the sprinkles can be rods, pearls, sequins, and more and come in a variety of colors.

Nonstick cooking spray

1½ cups all-purpose flour

¾ teaspoon baking powder

¼ teaspoon baking soda

¼ teaspoon salt

⅓ cup buttermilk

⅓ cup whole milk

6 tablespoons unsalted butter, at room temperature

½ cup sugar

1 large egg

2 teaspoons vanilla extract

3 tablespoons multicolored sprinkles, plus more for decorating

1 recipe Vanilla, Chocolate, or Strawberry Glaze (page 17)

Preheat the oven to 375°F. Coat the wells of a doughnut pan with nonstick cooking spray.

In a bowl, whisk together the flour, baking powder, baking soda, and salt. In a measuring cup, stir together the buttermilk and whole milk. Set aside.

In the bowl of a stand mixer fitted with the paddle attachment, beat the butter and sugar on medium speed until light and fluffy, about 2 minutes. Scrape down the sides of the bowl. Add the egg and vanilla; beat on medium speed until combined, about 1 minute. On low speed, add the flour mixture in 3 additions, alternating with the milk mixture and beginning and ending with the flour. Beat each addition until just blended. Fold in the sprinkles.

Pour 2 tablespoons batter into each prepared well. Bake, rotating the pan 180 degrees halfway through baking, until a toothpick inserted into the doughnuts comes out clean, about 10 minutes. Let cool in the pan on a cooling rack for 5 minutes, then invert the doughnuts onto the rack and let cool completely.

Meanwhile, wash and dry the pan and repeat to bake the remaining batter.

Line a baking sheet with parchment paper. Dip the doughnuts, top side down, into the glaze. Place, glazed side up, on the prepared baking sheet, decorate with sprinkles, and serve.

Vanilla Old-Fashioned Doughnuts

MAKES ABOUT · 10–12 · 3" DOUGHNUTS

Rich and a bit crumbly, cake doughnuts have a sturdier structure than yeast doughnuts, making them better candidates for coating with a glaze and topping with a garnish, such as toasted nuts or coconut.

3 cups all-purpose flour, plus more for dusting

1 teaspoon salt

1 teaspoon baking powder

½ teaspoon baking soda

¼ teaspoon ground nutmeg

2 tablespoons unsalted butter, melted and cooled

1 tablespoon vanilla extract

2 large eggs

½ cup buttermilk

½ cup granulated sugar

¼ cup firmly packed light brown sugar

Canola oil, for frying

1 recipe Vanilla Glaze or Chocolate Glaze (page 17)

In a bowl, whisk together the flour, salt, baking powder, baking soda, and nutmeg. In a measuring cup, stir together the butter and vanilla. Set aside.

In the bowl of a stand mixer fitted with the paddle attachment, beat together the eggs, buttermilk, and sugars on medium until well combined. Add the flour mixture and beat until just combined, then beat in the butter mixture until just combined.

Turn the dough out onto a well-floured surface and knead until the dough comes together. (The dough will be very sticky.) Roll out ½ inch thick. Using a doughnut cutter or 2 different-sized round cutters (3 inch and 1 inch), cut out doughnuts and holes. Transfer to a well-floured baking sheet and refrigerate for at least 30 minutes or up to 2 hours. Cut into old-fashioned shapes, if desired (see page 13).

To fry the doughnuts, see Successful Frying (page 14). Heat the oil over medium-high until it registers 360°F on a deep-frying thermometer. When the doughnuts are cooked through (cut one open to test), 1–2 minutes per side (holes take less time), use a slotted spoon to transfer to a cooling rack or prepared baking sheet. Let cool for 5 minutes. Dip the doughnuts, top side down, into the glaze and serve.

Chocolate Old-Fashioned Doughnuts

Traditionally ring shaped with jagged edges, old-fashioned doughnuts are cake doughnuts with a crispy, craggy exterior. This recipe skips over the plain old-fashioned for a rich chocolate version with a hint of mocha.

2½ cups all-purpose flour, plus more for dusting

1 cup cocoa powder

1 teaspoon salt

1 teaspoon baking powder

½ teaspoon baking soda

1½ teaspoons instant espresso powder

2 tablespoons unsalted butter, melted and cooled

1 tablespoons vanilla extract

2 large eggs

½ cup buttermilk

½ cup whole milk

¾ cup sugar

Canola oil, for frying

1 recipe Vanilla Glaze or Chocolate Glaze (page 17)

In a bowl, whisk together the flour, cocoa powder, salt, baking powder, and baking soda. In a measuring cup, stir together the espresso powder and 1 tablespoon water, then stir in the butter and vanilla. Set aside.

In the bowl of a stand mixer fitted with the paddle attachment, beat together the eggs, buttermilk, whole milk, and sugar on medium until well combined. Add the flour mixture and beat until just combined, then beat in the espresso mixture until just combined.

Turn the dough out onto a well-floured surface and knead until the dough comes together. (The dough will be very sticky.) Roll out ½ inch thick. Using a doughnut cutter or 2 different-sized round cutters (3 inch and 1 inch), cut out doughnuts and holes. Transfer to a well-floured baking sheet and refrigerate for at least 30 minutes or up to 2 hours. Cut into old-fashioned shapes, if desired (see page 13).

To fry the doughnuts, see Successful Frying (page 14). Heat the oil over medium-high until it registers 360°F on a deep-frying thermometer. When the doughnuts are cooked through (cut one open to test), 1–2 minutes per side (holes take less time), use a slotted spoon to transfer to the cooling rack or prepared baking sheet. Let cool for 5 minutes. Dip the doughnuts, top side down, into the glaze and serve.

Cinnamon Crumb Doughnuts

A buttery, sweet, slightly crunchy topping caps these old-fashioned baked doughnuts. For an earthier flavor, substitute ground cardamom for the cinnamon. If you like, dust the cooled doughnuts with confectioners' sugar.

FOR THE TOPPING

½ cup firmly packed light brown sugar

½ teaspoon ground cinnamon

Pinch of salt

6 tablespoons cold unsalted butter, cut into ¼-inch cubes

¾ cup all-purpose flour

FOR THE DOUGHNUTS

Nonstick cooking spray

1½ cups all-purpose flour

¾ teaspoon baking powder

¼ teaspoon baking soda

¼ teaspoon salt

⅓ cup buttermilk

⅓ cup whole milk

6 tablespoons unsalted butter, at room temperature

½ cup granulated sugar

1 large egg

2 teaspoons vanilla extract

To make the crumb topping, in a bowl, stir together the brown sugar, cinnamon, and salt. Using your fingertips or a pastry cutter, add the butter and the flour and mix well until pea-sized clumps form. Set aside.

To make the doughnuts, preheat the oven to 375°F. Coat the wells of a doughnut pan with nonstick cooking spray. In a bowl, whisk together the flour, baking powder, baking soda, and salt. In a measuring cup, stir together the buttermilk and whole milk. Set aside.

In the bowl of a stand mixer fitted with the paddle attachment, beat together the butter and granulated sugar on medium speed until light and fluffy, about 2 minutes. Scrape down the sides of the bowl. Add the egg and vanilla and beat on medium speed until combined, about 1 minute. On low speed, add the flour mixture in 3 additions, alternating with the milk mixture and beginning and ending with the flour. Beat each addition until just blended.

Pour 2 tablespoons batter into each prepared well. Sprinkle each with about 2 tablespoons topping. Bake, rotating the pan 180 degrees halfway through baking, until a toothpick inserted into the doughnuts comes out clean, about 10 minutes. Let cool in the pan on a cooling rack for 5 minutes, then invert the doughnuts onto the rack and let cool completely.

Meanwhile, wash and dry the pan and repeat to bake the remaining batter.

Strawberry Doughnuts

MAKES ABOUT • 16–18 • 3" DOUGHNUTS

To transform these pink-tinted confections into triple-strawberry doughnuts, fold ⅓ to ½ cup finely chopped strawberries into the glaze. Do not chop the berries in advance; they will weep and thin the glaze.

Nonstick cooking spray

2 cups fresh or frozen strawberries, quartered, thawed if frozen

1½ cups all-purpose flour

¾ teaspoon baking powder

¼ teaspoon baking soda

¼ teaspoon salt

⅓ cup plus 1 tablespoon buttermilk

6 tablespoons unsalted butter, at room temperature

½ cup sugar

1 large egg

2 teaspoons vanilla extract

1 recipe Strawberry Glaze (page 17)

Preheat the oven to 375°F. Coat the wells of a doughnut pan with nonstick cooking spray.

In a blender, purée the strawberries until smooth. Pour through a fine-mesh sieve into a saucepan. Simmer over medium heat until syrupy, 5–7 minutes. Let cool.

In a bowl, whisk together the flour, baking powder, baking soda, and salt. In a measuring cup, stir together the buttermilk and ⅓ cup of the strawberry syrup. The remaining syrup is used in the glaze. Set aside.

In the bowl of a stand mixer fitted with the paddle attachment, beat together the butter and sugar on medium speed until light and fluffy, about 2 minutes. Scrape down the sides of the bowl. Add the egg and vanilla and beat on medium speed until combined, about 1 minute. On low speed, add the flour mixture in 3 additions, alternating with the buttermilk mixture and beginning and ending with the flour. Beat each addition until just blended.

Pour 2 tablespoons batter into each prepared well. Bake, rotating the pan 180 degrees halfway through baking, until a toothpick inserted into the doughnuts comes out clean, about 10 minutes. Let cool in the pan on a cooling rack for 5 minutes, then invert the doughnuts onto the rack and let cool completely.

Meanwhile, wash and dry the pan and repeat to bake the remaining batter. Dip the doughnuts, top side down, into the glaze and serve.

Lemon Doughnuts with Pistachios

You can use supermarket lemons—Lisbon or Eureka variety—for both the doughnut batter and the glaze, but if you prefer a less tart, more floral flavor, look for Meyer lemons at a farmers' markets or specialty stores.

FOR THE DOUGHNUTS
Nonstick cooking spray
½ cup granulated sugar
Zest and juice of 1 lemon
1½ cups all-purpose flour
¾ teaspoon baking powder
¼ teaspoon baking soda
¼ teaspoon salt
⅓ cup buttermilk
⅓ cup whole milk
6 tablespoons
unsalted butter, at
room temperature
1 large egg
2 teaspoons vanilla extract

FOR THE GLAZE
½ cup plain Greek yogurt
or other whole milk yogurt
Zest of 1 lemon
¼ teaspoon salt
1 cup confectioners' sugar

½ cup toasted pistachios,
chopped (optional)

To make the doughnuts, preheat the oven to 375°F. Coat the wells of a doughnut pan with nonstick cooking spray.

In a small bowl, combine the granulated sugar and lemon zest. Using your fingertips, rub the zest into the sugar. In another bowl, whisk together the flour, baking powder, baking soda, and salt. In a measuring cup, stir together the buttermilk, whole milk, and lemon juice.

In the bowl of a stand mixer fitted with the paddle attachment, beat together the sugar mixture and butter on medium speed until light and fluffy, about 2 minutes. Scrape down the sides of the bowl. Add the egg and vanilla and beat on medium speed until combined, about 1 minute.

On low speed, add the flour mixture in 3 additions, alternating with the milk mixture and beginning and ending with the flour. Beat each addition until just blended.

Pour 2 tablespoons batter into each prepared well. Bake, rotating the pan 180 degrees halfway through baking, until a toothpick inserted into the doughnuts comes out clean, about 10 minutes. Let cool in the pan on a cooling rack for 5 minutes, then invert the doughnuts onto the rack and let cool completely. Meanwhile, wash and dry the pan and repeat to bake the remaining batter.

To make the glaze, in a bowl, stir together the yogurt, lemon zest, and salt. Add the confectioners' sugar and stir until smooth and well blended. Dip the doughnuts, top side down, into the glaze, sprinkle with the pistachios, if using, and serve.

Peppermint Bark Chocolate Doughnuts

The best peppermint bark is a thin layer each of semisweet chocolate and white chocolate, with crushed peppermint candies studding the top. To infuse the doughnut batter with peppermint, add 1 teaspoon peppermint extract with the milk.

Nonstick cooking spray

1 cup plus 2 tablespoons all-purpose flour

½ cup cocoa powder

1½ teaspoons instant espresso powder (optional)

¾ teaspoon baking powder

¼ teaspoon baking soda

¼ teaspoon salt

⅓ cup buttermilk

⅓ cup whole milk

6 tablespoons unsalted butter, at room temperature

½ cup sugar

1 large egg

2 teaspoons vanilla extract

1 recipe Chocolate Glaze (page 17)

1 cup crushed peppermint bark or peppermint candies

Preheat the oven to 375°F. Coat the wells of a doughnut pan with nonstick cooking spray.

In a bowl, whisk together the flour, cocoa powder, espresso powder (if using), baking powder, baking soda, and salt. In a measuring cup, stir together the buttermilk and whole milk. Set aside.

In the bowl of a stand mixer fitted with the paddle attachment, beat together the butter and sugar on medium speed until light and fluffy, about 2 minutes. Scrape down the sides of the bowl. Add the egg and vanilla and beat on medium speed until combined, about 1 minute.

On low speed, add the flour mixture in 3 additions, alternating with the milk mixture and beginning and ending with the flour. Beat each addition until just blended.

Pour 2 tablespoons batter into each prepared well. Bake, rotating the pan 180 degrees halfway through baking, until a toothpick inserted into the doughnuts comes out clean, about 10 minutes. Let cool in the pan on a cooling rack for 5 minutes, then invert the doughnuts onto the rack and let cool completely.

Meanwhile, wash and dry the pan and repeat to bake the remaining batter.

Dip the doughnuts, top side down, into the glaze, sprinkle with the peppermint bark, and serve.

Pumpkin Doughnuts

On cool fall mornings, these spiced doughnuts, with their sunny orange, moist crumb, are a great pick-me-up. If you like, swap out the cinnamon-sugar topping for a pumpkin-friendly maple glaze (page 33).

FOR THE DOUGHNUTS

Nonstick cooking spray

1½ cups all-purpose flour

¾ teaspoon baking powder

¼ teaspoon *each* baking soda and salt

1½ teaspoons ground cinnamon

1 teaspoon *each* ground nutmeg and ground ginger

⅓ cup buttermilk

⅓ cup whole milk

½ cup pumpkin purée

Juice of 1 lemon

6 tablespoons unsalted butter, at room temperature

½ cup sugar

1 large egg

2 teaspoons vanilla extract

FOR THE TOPPING

⅔ cup sugar

2 teaspoons ground cinnamon

¼ teaspoon salt

½ cup unsalted butter

To make the doughnuts, preheat the oven to 375°F. Coat the wells of a doughnut pan with nonstick cooking spray.

In a bowl, whisk together the flour, baking powder, baking soda, salt, cinnamon, nutmeg, and ginger. In another bowl, stir together the buttermilk, milk, pumpkin purée, and lemon juice. Set aside.

In the bowl of a stand mixer fitted with the paddle attachment, beat together the butter and sugar on medium speed until light and fluffy, about 2 minutes. Scrape down the sides of the bowl. Add the egg and vanilla; beat on medium speed until combined, about 1 minute. On low speed, add the flour mixture in 3 additions, alternating with the buttermilk mixture and beginning and ending with the flour. Beat each addition until just blended.

Pour 2 tablespoons batter into each prepared well. Bake, rotating the pan 180 degrees halfway through baking, until a toothpick inserted into the doughnuts comes out clean, about 10 minutes. Let cool in the pan on a wire rack for 5 minutes, then invert the doughnuts onto the rack and let cool completely.

Meanwhile, wash and dry the pan and repeat to bake the remaining batter.

In a shallow bowl, stir together the sugar, cinnamon, and salt. In another bowl, melt the butter and let cool slightly. Dip the cooled doughnuts into the melted butter, then toss in the topping and serve.

Savory Cheesy-Jalapeño Doughnuts

Make these big-flavored doughnuts for your next casual weekend brunch. For a different national accent, substitute Italian fontina, Dutch Gouda, French Comté, or a young Spanish Manchego for the Cheddar.

Nonstick cooking spray

1½ cups all-purpose flour

1½ tablespoons sugar

¾ teaspoon baking powder

¼ teaspoon baking soda

½ teaspoon salt

½ cup buttermilk

⅓ cup plus 2 tablespoons whole milk

6 tablespoons unsalted butter, melted and cooled

1 large egg

¼ cup thinly sliced green onion

½ jalapeño chile, seeded and diced

¾ cup shredded Cheddar cheese

Preheat the oven to 375°F. Coat the wells of a doughnut pan with nonstick cooking spray. Line a baking sheet with parchment paper.

In a large bowl, whisk together the flour, sugar, baking powder, baking soda, and salt. In another bowl, whisk together the buttermilk, whole milk, butter, and egg. Add the milk mixture to the flour mixture, stirring until just combined. Fold in the green onion, jalapeño, and ½ cup of the cheese.

Pour 2 tablespoons batter into each prepared well. Bake, rotating the pan 180 degrees halfway through baking, until a toothpick inserted into the doughnuts comes out clean, about 10 minutes. Immediately invert the doughnuts onto the prepared baking sheet. Wash and dry the pan and repeat to bake the remaining batter.

Turn the oven to broil. Sprinkle the remaining ¼ cup cheese over the doughnuts. Broil until melted and golden brown, about 1 minute. Serve right away.

Index

THE DOUGHNUT COOKBOOK

Conceived and produced by Weldon Owen
In collaboration with Williams Sonoma, Inc.
3250 Van Ness Avenue, San Francisco, CA 94109

A WELDON OWEN PRODUCTION

1045 Sansome Street, Suite 100
San Francisco, CA 94111
www.weldonowen.com

Copyright © 2016 Weldon Owen, Inc.
and Williams Sonoma, Inc.
All rights reserved, including the right of
reproduction in whole or in part in any form.

Printed in China

First printed in 2016
12 11 10 9

Library of Congress Cataloging-in-Publication
data is available.

ISBN 978-1-68188-134-8

WELDON OWEN, INC.

President & Publisher Roger Shaw
SVP, Sales & Marketing Amy Kaneko
Finance & Operations Director Philip Paulick

Associate Publisher Amy Marr
Associate Editor Emma Rudolph

Creative Director Kelly Booth
Art Director Marisa Kwek
Senior Production Designer Rachel Lopez Metzger

Production Director Chris Hemesath
Associate Production Director Michelle Duggan
Imaging Manager Don Hill

Photographer Eva Kolenko
Food Stylist Fanny Pan
Prop Stylist Natasha Kolenko

ACKNOWLEDGMENTS

Weldon Owen wishes to thank the following people for their
generous support in producing this book: Kris Balloun, Gloria Geller,
Amy Hatwig, Elizabeth Parson, Sharon Silva, and Emily Stewart.